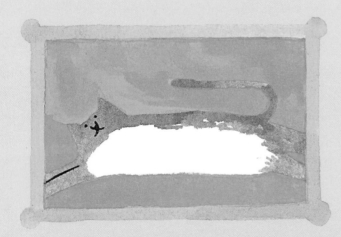

why do cats meow?

why do cats meow?

**Curious questions about
your favorite pet**

Illustrated by Lily Snowden-Fine
Cat expert Dr. Nick Crumpton

Contents

Lions in your living room

How long have people kept pet cats?

People have kept cats as pets for more than 3,500 years, but they first started living alongside humans over 9,000 years ago. Some scientists think that today there might be 1 billion domestic cats in the world—that's one cat for every eight people!

One big litter
The domestic cat is just one of 40 species, but all of them, whether big or small, wild or domestic, are part of the same family.

Wild at heart
Domestic cats haven't changed very much from the wild animals they were 9,000 years ago. This is why they are much better at looking after themselves than dogs.

Cats and their pet humans
Rather than humans choosing to turn cats into tame pets, cats probably domesticated themselves as they spent time around humans (and our tasty dinners).

The good, the bad and the snuggly

How many different cats are there?

Although all domestic cats are the same species, they can look quite different. Only 2% of the world's cats are "pure" breeds and that is because cats choose their own mates. Most cats are a mix of different breeds. Some cat experts consider there to be 40 breeds, while others recognize over 80!

Tall tails
The world's longest cat tail, at almost 18 inches long, belongs to Cygnus Regulus Powers, a silver Maine Coon cat.

Small tails
Manx cats and long-haired Cymric cats have no tails—or at least very stubby ones. The Japanese Bobtail has a short, fluffy tail that looks like a little pom-pom.

Curl craze!
In the 1980s, having big, curly human hair was very fashionable. LaPerm cats are named after their curly coats which resemble a perm. In addition to looking fabulous, they also have very friendly personalities.

Under-fur heating
Sphynx cats are either entirely bald or covered only in very fine hairs. Because they have hardly any fur, their body loses heat quickly (which means they're warm to hold).

Making their mark

Do cats have territories?

Cats are very territorial, which means they claim areas of land as their own and will often fight off intruders. They choose areas that may be excellent sources of food, or great places to nap in, so their owner's home is definitely part of their territory.

Guarding the garden
To make sure other cats don't sneak into their territory, cats patrol and re-mark their areas regularly.

Some cats will share their territory, with one cat controlling it in the morning and another cat taking it over for the afternoon.

Tag—you're mine!
Cats claim objects as part of their territory by scratching, rubbing against or peeing on them. This spreads their scent so other cats know to "stay out."

Near or far
A male cat tends to have a larger territory than a female. Cats often have small territories when there is lots of food around and large territories when it's slim pickings!

You belong to me
Cats have scent glands over many parts of their bodies. When they head-butt and rub their face against your leg, they are leaving their scent on you (as well as trying to grab your attention).

How to speak cat

Why do cats meow?

When a cat "meows" to its owner it can mean a lot of different things from "hello," "I want to play" to "I want to go outside."

Two for one

Cats can purr at two days old. When they combine a purr with a meow it usually means they want your attention... and they are hungry!

12

Chatty cats
Siamese cats are one of the noisiest breeds and will chatter away all day long to their owners. Maine Coon cats can make a chirping sound (often at birds they can see outside).

Meow meanings
Cats can make about 100 different sounds, which all mean different things. A hiss tells you to "go away," and a purr tells you they trust you.

Hello, Kitty
Although it is their most famous call, only kittens meow at other cats (to let their mother know they are cold or hungry). Adult cats only meow at humans.

Feeling the way

What do a cat's whiskers do?

Domestic cats do most of their hunting at dawn and dusk. It is difficult to see well at these times of the day so they rely on their whiskers to help them move and hunt instead.

Hair everywhere!

A cat doesn't just have whiskers on either side of its mouth, it also has them on its ears, above its eyes and on its front legs.

Fully adjustable

Whiskers can be held flat against a cat's face, pushed forwards, or spread outward depending on whether it is feeling happy, content, curious or anxious.

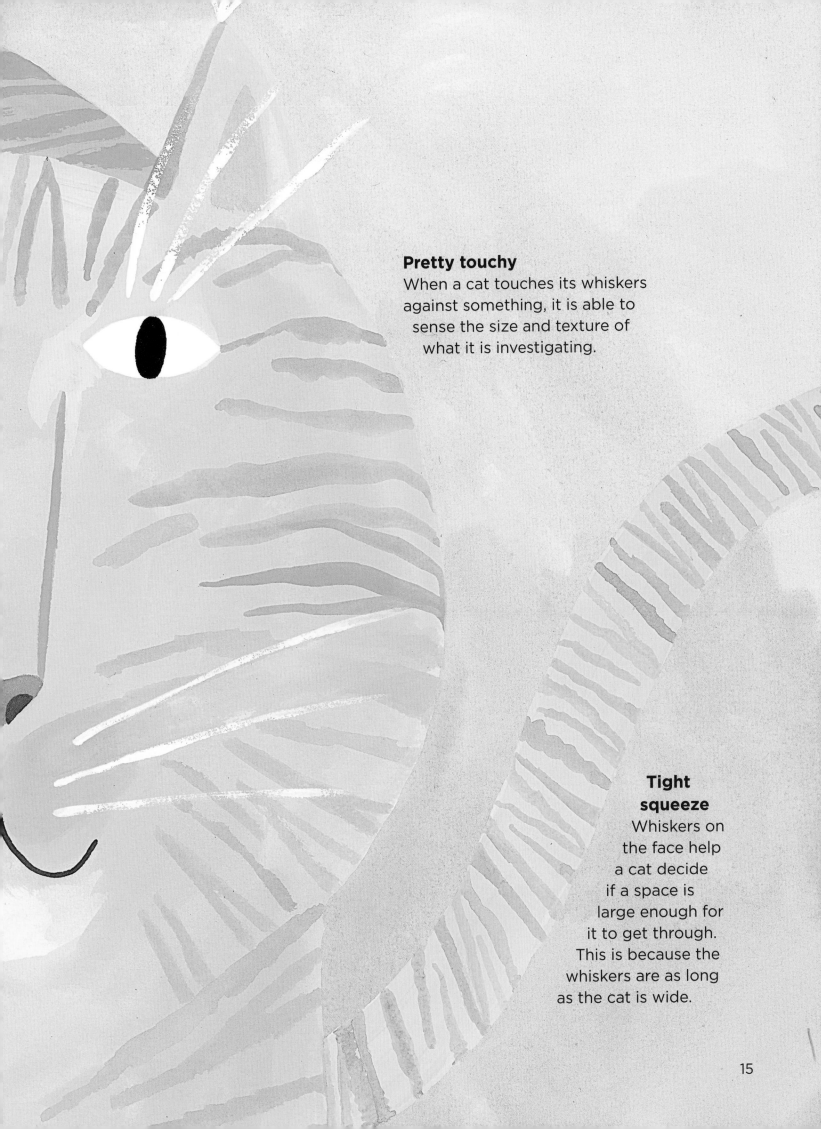

Pretty touchy
When a cat touches its whiskers against something, it is able to sense the size and texture of what it is investigating.

Tight squeeze
Whiskers on the face help a cat decide if a space is large enough for it to get through. This is because the whiskers are as long as the cat is wide.

15

Following your nose

Why do cats have wet noses?

Cats have wet noses to help regulate their body temperature. Scent particles also stick better to a wet nose which improves their sense of smell. A dry nose can mean a cat is sick but it can also mean it's been lying in the sun for too long!

A unique sniffer
Just like a human fingerprint, every cat's nose is unique, but you can only see the differences under a microscope.

Super smellers
A cat has a better sense of smell than a human and some smells like catnip are feline favorites. Smells from frying onions and perfume can be too strong for their sensitive noses though!

Blind and deaf

When a kitten is born it
is unable to see or hear.
Instead, it relies on its
sense of smell as well
as its sense of touch.

Smell the difference

Although a dog has more scent
receptors in its nose, a cat
can actually tell the difference
between a greater variety of
smells, even those very similar
to each other.

17

Witches and omens

Do cats bring bad luck?

All around the world, and for thousands of years, humans have had superstitions about cats. Some cultures believe cats bring bad luck, and some believe the opposite!

Supernatural sìth
The Cat Sìth is a fairy creature in Scottish mythology that appears as a black cat with a white mark on its chest, and was believed to steal people's souls.

Angel or demon
In Western Europe and the U.S., black cats are considered bad omens, but in Japan and parts of the UK it is thought to be a good sign if a black cat crosses your path.

Salty sea cats
Cats were believed to be able to protect ships at sea and some fishermen believed that their ship's cat could predict whether storms were on the horizon.

Come on in
In Japan, small sculptures of a Japanese Bobtail called a *maneki-neko*, or "beckoning cat," have been kept by people for almost 200 years and are believed to bring good luck.

What a cat sees

Can cats see in the dark?

Twilight is a difficult time to move around and hunt in, but cats have lots of tricks to help them peer through the darkness.

Light fantastic

Like many other mammals, the back of cats' eyes are reflective, which allows their eyes to capture more light to see by at night.

Eye on the prize

Cats don't need to blink their eyes to keep them wet as often as humans do. This means they can keep their gaze fixed on their prey.

Cat colors

Cats can't see all of the colors that humans can see, but they can see more shades of red and green than dogs can.

Widescreen vision
Cats have a wider field of vision than humans. This means they can see things moving "in the corner of their eye" better than people.

21

Petting your pet

Do cats like being stroked?

Cats groom and rub against each other as a sign of affection, so stroking your cat is a good way to form a close bond with your pet. Watch where you stroke though, as there are some areas like tails or tummies that are usually off limits!

Where's best

Cats like to be stroked best on the places where they have lots of scent glands, like on their chin and between their ears.

Calming cats

Stroking cats relaxes humans and if a cat slowly blinks, rubs its head against the person stroking it or holds its tail up high, it's having a great time too!

How do you do?
When a cat meets another cat they communicate by rubbing against each other in the same places they like to be stroked.

Not for every cat
Some breeds of cat, like the floppy Ragdoll cat, love being stroked, but some don't, so it's important to pay attention to how a cat responds to being fussed over.

Wary of the water

Why don't cats like water?

The first domestic cats were from Africa and the Middle East, which are dry places, and most of today's cats still have their ancestors' distrust of water and getting wet.

Turkish baths

The Turkish Van breed is nicknamed the "swimming cat" because it loves to dabble and even swim in water thanks to its thick, water-repellent coat.

Under the tap

Although they dislike getting wet, cats are often obsessed with running faucets. This is possibly because the movement of the water triggers their hunting reflexes. Maine Coons have a reputation for learning to turn the tap on.

Dry clean only

Most cats don't like getting their hair wet. Wet fur is much harder to groom and keep clean.

An appetite for destruction

Why do cats like scratching things?

Cats like scratching carpets, furniture and scratching posts because it helps remove the dead, outer "sheath" layer of their claws. This keeps them short and exposes sharper, newly grown claws beneath.

Surveying their kingdom

Sharp claws let cats hang from great heights, like the upper reaches of your curtains, which they love to climb in order to reach a high, safe vantage point to look down from.

Scratch 'n' sniff

Cats have scent glands on their paws, so by scratching they are transferring their own particular smell onto things.

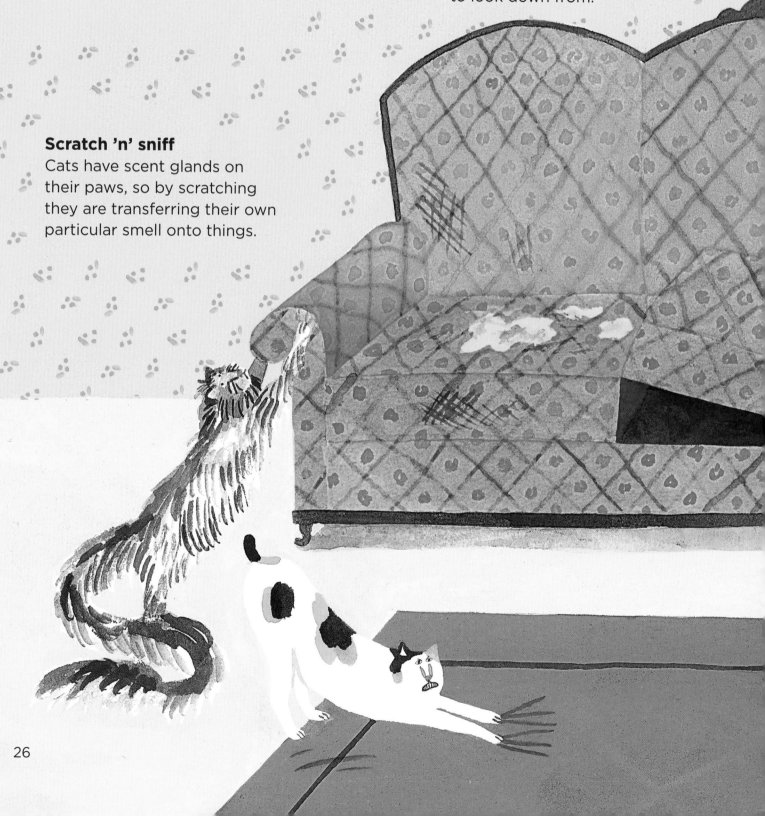

Concealed weapons
Unlike dogs, domestic cats can retract most of their claws, which helps them tread quietly and keep their claws safe from harm.

Freaky feet
Most cats have 18 toes, with five on each front paw, and four on each hind paw, but some cats have extra toes on their front paws. These are called Polydactyl cats.

27

Unbreakable

Do cats have nine lives?

The story that cats have nine lives isn't really true, but fearless felines have some amazing behaviors and body-secrets that help them survive catastrophes.

Bounce back

When falling a short distance, cats' long, spring-like legs absorb lots of energy when they touch down which keeps them from getting injured.

Four to the floor

Cats usually land on their feet from great heights due to their very flexible extra-long spine, which allows them to twist quickly before reaching the ground.

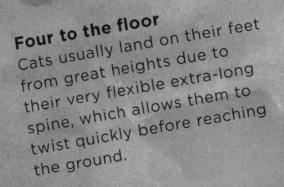

Free-falling

If a cat is falling from a great height, it spreads out its legs to slow its fall. This trick means cats fall at only half the speed a human would.

Cat years

The average life expectancy of a house cat is just over 15 years, although the oldest cat ever recorded reached the ripe old age of 38!

Cranky kitties

Is my cat ignoring me?

Unlike humans, cats don't communicate using their facial features, which can make them look like they're in their own little world for much of the time. But cats are usually very aware of what's happening around them.

Homing in

Cats have over 30 muscles in their ears. This allows them to move each ear independently, which helps them work out where noises come from.

Pardon me-ow?

A few cats are born deaf: cats with white coats and blue eyes have a greater chance of being completely deaf.

Highs and lows
Cats have a great sense of hearing and can hear higher-pitched sounds three times better than humans.

Music snobs
Cats like music, but only music specially composed at higher frequencies than humans can hear! Rumor has it that this music sounds a bit like purring and birdsong.

Celestial creatures

Where were cats worshipped?

The people who live on the banks of the River Nile and the icy fjords of Norway have incorporated cats into their beliefs for thousands of years.

Honored in death
Many pet cats were mummified after they died in ancient Egypt, which would have been very expensive for their owners but was a sign of great respect for the cat!

God of many
In 1,500 BCE, the cat-headed goddess Bastet was worshipped as the protector of women during pregnancy and childbirth, the protector of pharaohs and even as the goddess of music.

Skaukatt! Giddy up!
Two Norwegian Forest cats feature in Norse mythology as the *skaukatts* who can climb straight up sheer rock faces and who pull the Norse goddess Freya's chariot.

Holy protector
Shashthi is the Hindu goddess of childbirth and the protector of children. Her *vahana*, or mount, is a giant cat!

Cats in high places

Could cats rule the world?

From high politics to exposing academic scoundrels, these cats have strolled into high society and survived military mishaps.

STUBBS

The Honorable Stubbs

Stubbs was elected Honorary Mayor by the humans of Talkeetna in Alaska and held office for 19 years until he died in 2017.

AMBASSADOR

Parliament pets

Other cats in politics include Ambassador, who lives in the Ministry of Foreign Affairs in Kiev, Ukraine, and Larry, Chief Mouser to the Cabinet Office, who lives and works at 10 Downing Street in London.

LARRY

TARA

Cats vs. dogs

Tara "The Hero Cat" saved her family's child in 2014 when their neighbor's dog attacked him—a feat for which she was awarded the Blue Tiger Award, usually only given to military dogs.

TRIM

DR. ZOE D. KATZE

Ship-shape

Trim was the first cat to travel all the way around Australia with the crew of the HMS *Investigator* in 1803, and was a hardy ship's cat who survived falling overboard as a kitten after being born at sea.

Clever cat?

Dr. Zoe D. Katze received a PhD in hypnotherapy with her human's help and by doing so helped expose organizations giving away academic awards to anyone who could afford to buy them!

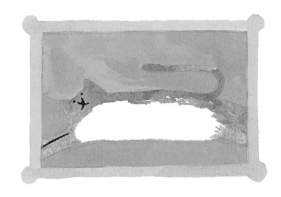

Hunting instinct

Why do cats bring us dead animals?

Cats bring home dead or injured prey to teach young cats how to catch food. They sometimes leave them for their owners because they think you can't catch prey either!

Slice-and-dice
Cats, unlike dogs, do not have wide, back molars suitable for crunching food. Cats' teeth are thin and blade-like for slicing through meat.

Creatures of habit

Hunting is a natural behavior for cats, but their human owners can help save wild animals by keeping their cats indoors more and playing with them to help redirect their killer instinct.

What a rush

Hunting is exciting for cats and after catching their prey they often have to "take a walk" to calm down and prepare themselves for eating.

Unwanted gifts

All cats are carnivores and eat almost only meat, which, in the wild, means hunting for their food. Pet cats still have this instinct so they sometimes can't resist catching small animals.

Family matters

When do cats have kittens?

Female cats are excellent mothers and can begin to have kittens when they are less than a year old. Domestic cats can become pregnant at any time, but most owners choose to have their pets neutered to guard against any unplanned parenting!

Express delivery
Whereas human pregnancies last for nine months, cats are only pregnant for roughly two—between 63 and 67 days.

Showing signs
It can be very difficult to tell when a cat is pregnant, but if she begins vomiting in the morning, has a bigger appetite, and is more affectionate than usual, the chances are she's carrying kittens!

Privacy, please
Cat mothers usually want to look after their young on their own and don't like humans interfering, so pregnant mothers often sneak away to have their kittens in private.

Counting kittens
The average number of kittens in a litter is between three and six, although it is possible for some cats to give birth to more than 15!

39

Clean freaks

Why do cats lick their own butts?

Cats spend up to a quarter of the hours that they are awake licking themselves. This keeps them clean, makes sure that their coat is not ruffled (which helps keep them warm), and releases more scent from their scent glands.

Head-to-tail
Cats always groom their bodies in a specific order:

1
Lick their lips

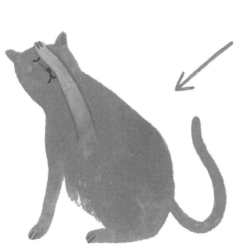

2
Lick the side of one paw

3
Rub this paw over their head (including the eye, ear and chin)

Sharp tongues
Cats' tongues are covered in little hooks, which act like the teeth of a comb to brush parasites and dirt from their fur.

4
Do the same with the other paw on the other side of the face

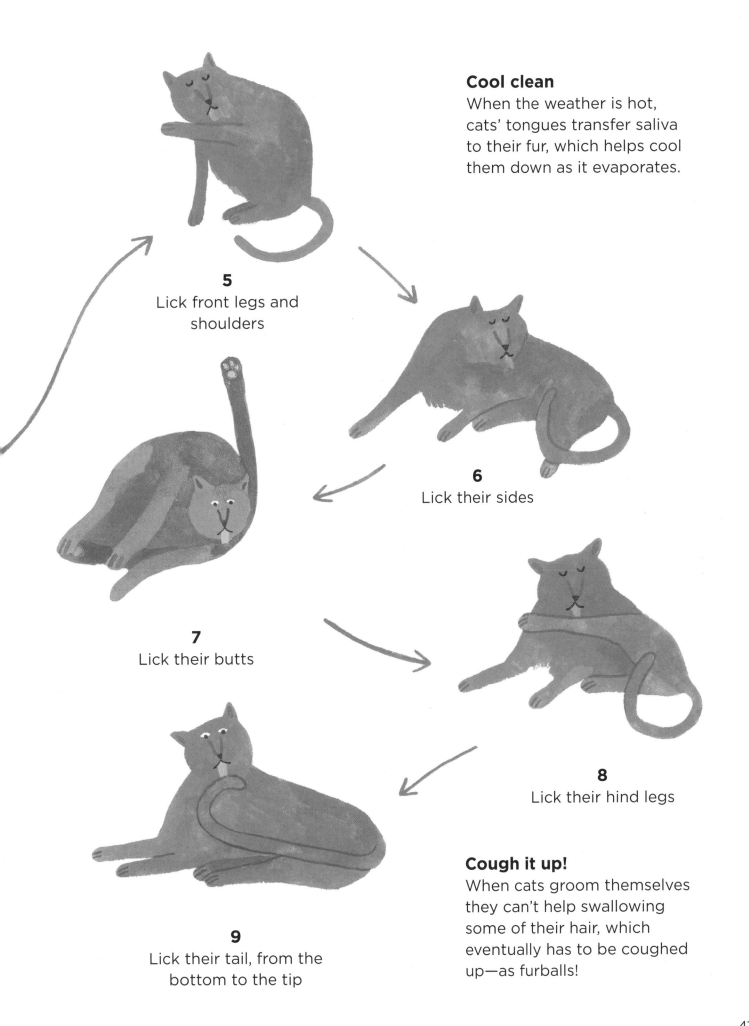

Cool clean
When the weather is hot, cats' tongues transfer saliva to their fur, which helps cool them down as it evaporates.

5
Lick front legs and shoulders

6
Lick their sides

7
Lick their butts

8
Lick their hind legs

9
Lick their tail, from the bottom to the tip

Cough it up!
When cats groom themselves they can't help swallowing some of their hair, which eventually has to be coughed up—as furballs!

Content as can be

How can you keep your cat healthy?

Cat owners need to make sure their cat is active and eats well, so that it can live a long and happy life. Always register your cat with a vet and remember to make sure it has been microchipped so it can be traced back to you if it gets lost!

Saucer of bleurgh!
Surprisingly, most cats are lactose intolerant, which means that giving them milk can make them sick.

Fat cats
A lazy cat that eats too much and doesn't exercise is in danger of becoming very unhealthy, so make sure you play with your cat every day to keep it active.

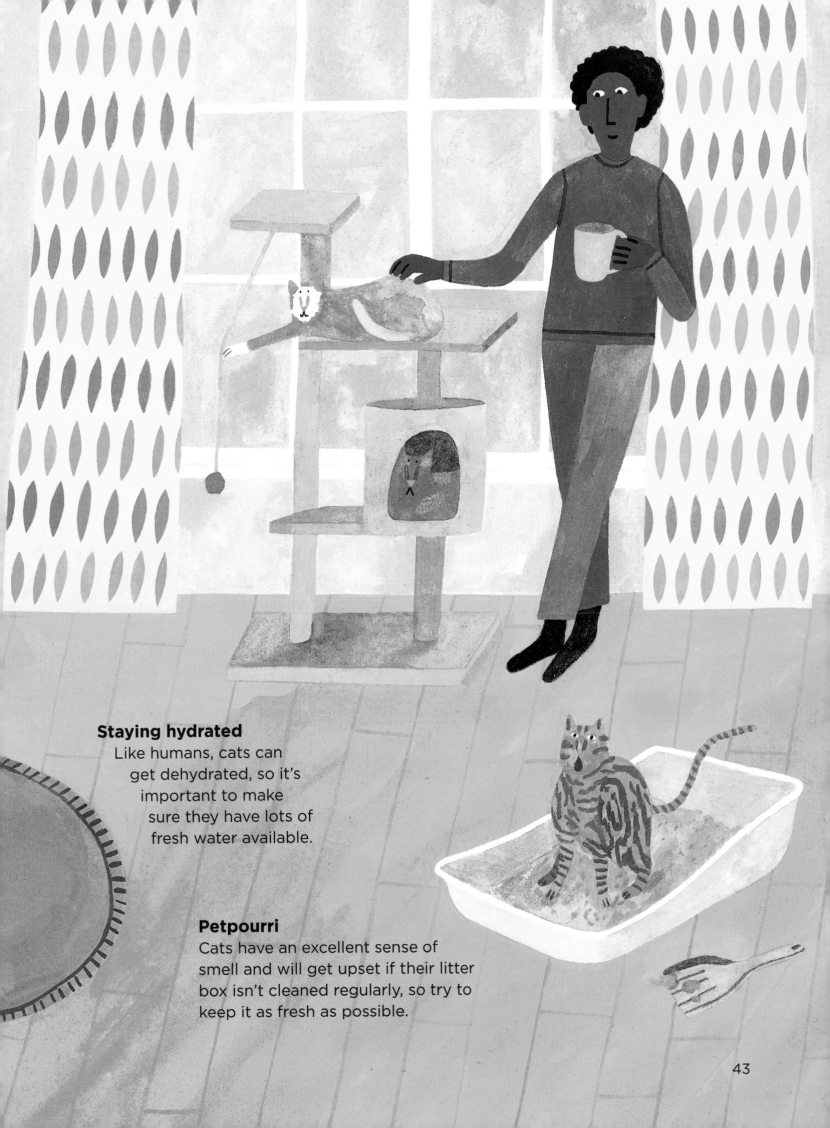

Staying hydrated
Like humans, cats can get dehydrated, so it's important to make sure they have lots of fresh water available.

Petpourri
Cats have an excellent sense of smell and will get upset if their litter box isn't cleaned regularly, so try to keep it as fresh as possible.

Cat words

Carnivores – animals that eat meat.

Dehydrated – when the body doesn't have enough water in it, meaning that it can't function properly.

Domestic – when an animal is tame and kept by humans as a pet.

Domesticated – when an animal has learned to live comfortably in the presence of humans.

Grooming – when an animal cleans and takes care of its fur by licking it.

Hunting reflexes – built-in instincts that some animals have, which cause them to chase and kill other animals in order to eat them.

Instincts – actions that humans and animals do naturally, without thinking about them.

Life expectancy – the average number of years an animal is expected to live.

Litter (kittens) – a group of young kittens born to a mother cat all at the same time.

Molar – the big teeth at the back of human and some animals' mouths.

Microchip – a tiny electronic chip that is placed under the skin of a cat (or other animal) in order to identify or locate it if it gets lost.

Neuter – when a cat is neutered, it undergoes an operation to stop it from being able to have kittens.

Species – a group of animals that look and act like each other. Dogs and cats are different species, as are humans and chimpanzees.

Territorial – when an animal is possessive over a certain piece of land that they use.

Territory – the land that an animal has marked out for itself.

Index

Why do cats meow? © 2020 Thames & Hudson Ltd, London
Illustrations © 2020 Lily Snowden-Fine

Text by Nick Crumpton
Designed by Emily Sear

First published in 2020 in the United States of America by
Thames & Hudson Inc., 500 Fifth Avenue, New York, New York 10110

Reprinted 2020

Library of Congress Control Number 2020930575

ISBN 978-0-500-65238-1

Printed and bound in China by Shanghai Offset Printing Products Limited

Be the first to know about our new releases,
exclusive content and author events by visiting
thamesandhudson.com
thamesandhudsonusa.com
thamesandhudson.com.au